# Make M
# Beans & Peas



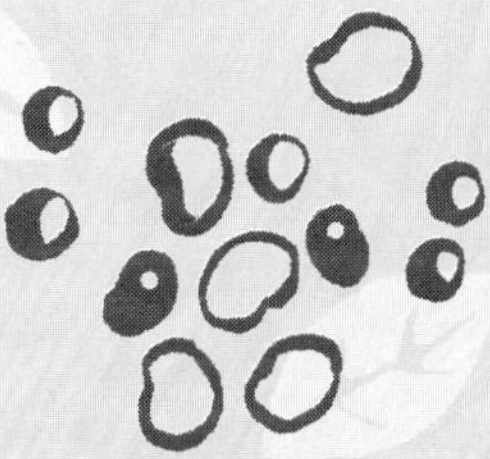

Patricia Harbottle

•

Peter Chadwick

•

Elisabeth Winkler

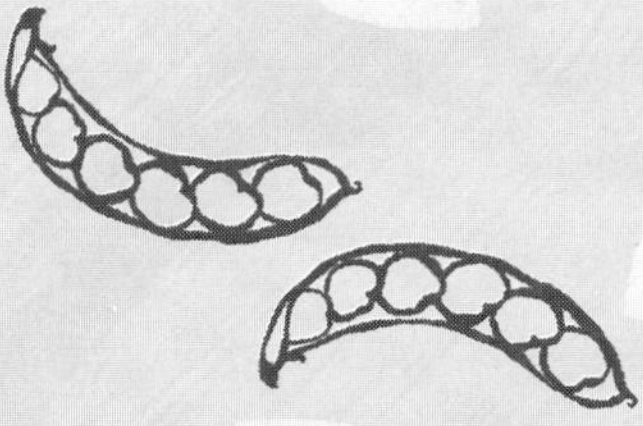

**Make More of Beans & Peas**


ISBN: 978-1-906316-27-3.



Published in 2009 by HotHive Books, Evesham, UK.
www.thehothive.com



A CIP record of this book is available from The British Library.



Printed in the UK by TJ International, Padstow.

hothivebooks

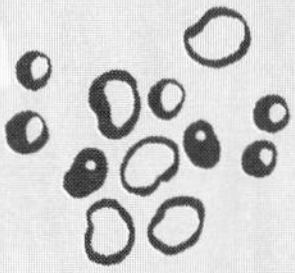

# About the authors

• • •

**Patricia Harbottle**'s lifelong love of the culinary arts climaxed with the establishment of her thriving catering enterprise in London; latterly she created a highly successful wine-related business. On moving to Dorset she pursued her interest in food, from its provenance, production and preparation to its presentation.

**Peter Chadwick** has been a horticultural explorer for over 40 years and his professional life is involved with the field scale production of vegetables. He lives in Worcestershire and plays the saxophone when he is not growing crops.

**Elisabeth Winkler** is passionate about eating for health. What could be more brimming with goodness than fresh produce you have grown yourself? Editor of the Soil Association magazine, *Living Earth*, for seven years, she is now food editor for the green magazine, *The Source*. Elisabeth's food blog (realfoodlover.wordpress.com) was shortlisted for the 2009 Guild of Food Writers Awards.

# Patricia's thank yous

• • •

**Michelle**. I have known Michelle Berriedale-Johnson for over 30 years. She and I set up a catering company in London – Catercall – in the 1970s, building it up into a thriving operation until we sold it to take up other interests. She is the author of numerous cookery books, including two for the British Museum, and the Editor of the only English magazine for allergy problems – *Foods Matter*. Check out her website www.foodsmatter.com.

**Anna del Conte** is a household name to anyone remotely interested in cooking. She is the queen of Italian cookery writers. I got to know her while living in London, and much better once we moved to live near each other in the country. It was she who had the idea for this series and graciously allowed us to take on the task of producing the books for it. Her recent book, *Amaretto, Apple Cake and Artichokes* (Vintage), is a delight.

**Mario** is a great friend who has been looking after my hair for nearly 40 years. He is half Italian, half Greek. A wonderful combination from every point of view, especially culinary. When he heard I was writing the recipes for this book he got very excited and asked his lovely English wife, Judy, to send me his favourite bean recipe.

**Gloria**. A few years ago I decided to attend a bread-making course in Dorset run by master baker Paul Merry. I soon became firm friends with him and his Chilean wife, Gloria. They are both excellent cooks. Gloria's bean salad is one of my favourites.

**Jen**. My wonderfully inspirational American friend, Jennifer Bushman, culinary author, cookery school creator and TV personality is a tower of strength and support in my creative efforts. Her intriguing recipes throughout this series will become favourite dishes for many.

# Foreword

## by Anna Del Conte

• • •

Whenever I had a meal at the Harbottles, I noticed that the vegetables were never treated just as an accompaniment to the meat or fish. They were never served just like that – plain steamed or boiled. They were always properly cooked and even more properly finished off; a treat in their own right.

So when Pat Harbottle told me that she was going to write a series of books on vegetables, I knew that all the recipes would be winners. I would no longer have to ask Pat, "And do you mind telling me how you cook those delicious beans?" But what I didn't know was how comprehensive this little book, the first of the series, would be. It is dedicated to beans and peas, in all their varieties and shapes: how to plant and grow them from seed; how to feed and nurture them; how to store them; and finally how to cook them.

The cultivating section of the book has been written by Peter Chadwick and Elisabeth Winkler, who manage to spell out very clearly anything and everything you need or want to know about the technical side of growing the vegetables, plus how, where and when to buy and what to look for when doing so.

The 50 recipes that follow are a joy to read and I am sure an even bigger joy to eat. Some are of utter simplicity, such as the green bean and olive salad – so reminiscent of the slopes of Vesuvius – or the peas with mint, garlic and lemon butter. Others are more sophisticated, such as the mouthwatering roulade of peas and prawns or the salad of mangetout, quail's egg, ricotta and tomato.

I was particularly captivated by the section of one-pot dishes, which I love to cook not only because the end result is delicious in its balance of flavours and perfect in its balance of nutrients, but also because of the saving of the attention necessary to look after two pots at the same time and of labour in the final washing up! I was tickled when I read Pat's instructions to save the liquid in which the vegetables have been boiled; the instructions of a thrifty, old-fashioned cook – and a cook after my own heart.

I am now longing to see the books that will follow: spuds and other roots; all sorts of greens and leaves, and what else? I shall become a complete vegetarian!

Anna Del Conte, May 2009, Dorset

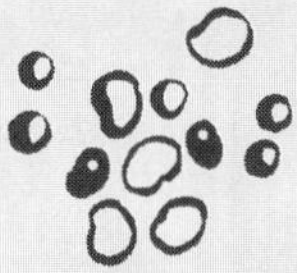

# Contents

• • •

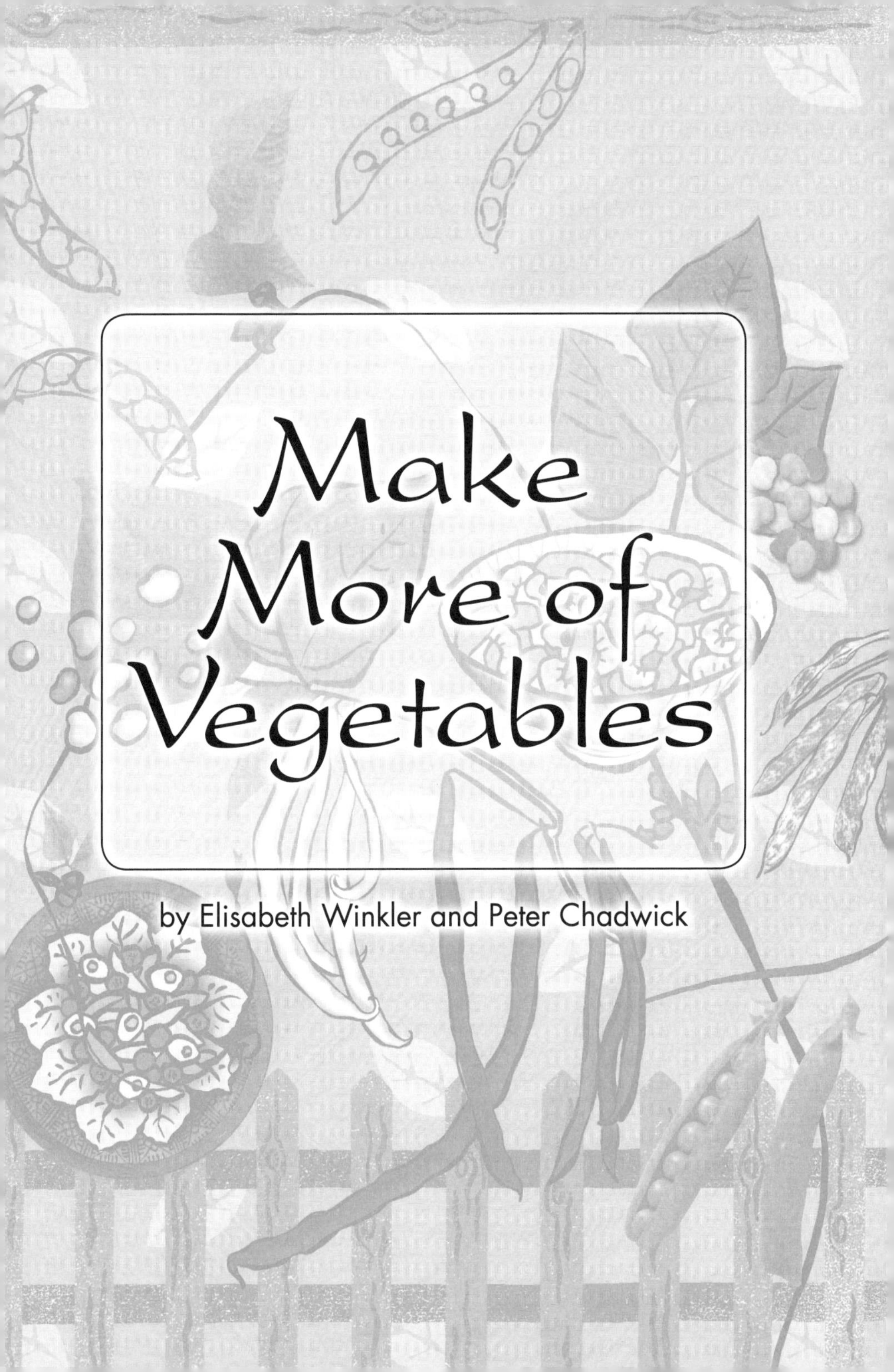

# Make More of Vegetables

by Elisabeth Winkler and Peter Chadwick

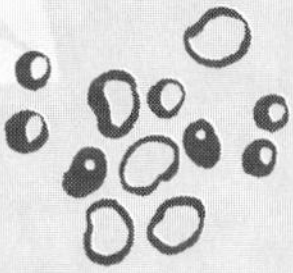

# Introduction

• • •

**The vegetable is a star.**
**Beautiful and vibrant,**
**it brings magical freshness**
**to the table.**

Mainstay of most of the globe's diet, vegetables are at the heart of good food, providing a diverse range of taste, colour and nutritional zing. Each book in this series puts a different group of vegetables in the spotlight with enticing recipes for the good-enough cook, and a guide on how (if you fancy) to grow your own.

You've heard of five-a-day. Nutritional warriors, vegetables support digestion, repair tissue and boost the immune system. Eating a range of vegetables helps guard against diet-linked diseases such as heart disease, some cancers and obesity. Vegetables are good for us and cheap compared to meat. Making sure they make up a half of a dish lowers its cost and boosts its health factor.

We know vegetables are good for us so how can we make more of them? These vivacious recipes combine interesting ingredients, including meat, to make temptingly tasty vegetable-based dishes.

The other beauty of vegetables is that they can be grown at home. You can't say that about many other foods. Many great cooks value fresh vegetables. Well, the best quality comes from your backyard. Each book in this series shows how to grow one type of vegetable from seed – enough to keep your family in, say, fresh beans, all summer long.

We are starting from scratch. Growing from seed brings a sense of achievement and a life-skill. This act of self-sufficiency brings satisfaction and confidence. Can we grow our own food? Yes, we can. If you are a first-time gardener or have been disappointed by your attempts so far, then this book is for you. Please read our growing guide without any pressure – because day-dreaming is the start of any adventure.

## Benefits of growing

It's a miracle to see a living thing grow from seed and evolve into a food-bearing plant. You feel more connected to nature, sunlight and the weather. It's helpful to ask: "What does this living thing need to thrive?" and see things from its perspective: warmth, water, good soil. You develop a relationship with your plants. Called husbandry, which means looking after, being attentive is more important than buying new garden tools.

You may want to invite your children and others to be part of this growing adventure. People of all ages can share the experience of sowing seeds in small pots of soil and waiting for the first growth. Once the seedlings are old enough to be planted out, the responsibility for watering them or picking the harvest can also be shared. Each member of the family could have one plant each to tend. Growing crops is a communal affair and brings people together for a common purpose.

Children love having something to look after and a plant helps develop that caretaking instinct. It's also educational, a chance to learn biology – the science of life. It's practical because the lesson will lead to food on the table. Involving children in growing their own has turned many a refusenik into a vegetable-lover, according to school food educationalists.

It's thrilling when your seeds grow into plants, in turn producing new seeds and pods for you to eat. Try eating a vegetable at different stages of its growth, as fresh as it can be. Broad beans picked when not much bigger than pea pods, for example, are delicious steamed whole but rarely offered for sale at that size.

Get ready for 12 plants grown from seed to enter your life. The grower, Peter Chadwick, and I will give easy-to-follow steps on how to create vegetable producing plants from seed. We are focusing on one vegetable group per book – keeping it simple.

## Why garden organically?

I don't want to blind you with data and science. As the organic farmer, Elliot Coleman, wrote in *The New Organic Grower's Four Season Harvest* (Green Publishing Company, 1992): "Organic methods are simpler and work better…Organic gardening is a great adventure, an expedition into a deeper and more satisfying understanding of vegetable production. You are now a participant rather than a spectator. You share creation."

Here are a few organic tips:

- The plant needs the soil for water and food. Look after your soil and the plant can look after itself;
- Put back into the soil what the growing plant takes out of it;
- Feed the soil with naturally made fertilisers such as compost or seaweed. Chemical feed is not as effective;
- Welcome the insects that eat the pests on your plant. If you use chemical sprays you will kill the pest-hunters too; and
- Your growing plants are living things in your care. Husbandry means just that – looking after.

## Shopping for veg at its best

When shopping, only the freshest vegetable will do. When a vegetable looks tired, limp, lacking in vitality, it is usually past its nutritional best. Seek crispness and brightness of colour. Being aware of the seasons will influence how and where you shop for this best veg. Eating seasonally is an adventure that leads to a different way of eating. You shop according to what is in season rather than what's on your vegetable shopping list.

Seasonality is less obvious when shopping in supermarkets, which offer a 'perpetual summer' with imports from countries with sun. I am not complaining – how could I live without chocolate, coffee or bananas? But when it comes to produce that grows in the UK, don't miss out on native veg and the chance to support its growers. Thanks to the public's growing demand, supermarkets are now selling more UK-grown vegetables in season.

During the winter we eat vegetables that store well, such as squashes, onions, potatoes, beetroot and carrots. Some farmers also grow fresh greens, cauliflower, pak choi or broccoli in winter. There is a lull towards the end of March, the 'hungry gap', when we are waiting for the spring sun to start off the new crop. As spring becomes summer, we enjoy a rich and seemingly endless harvest of fresh native vegetables right through until late autumn. Make the most of our home grown produce by buying local and seasonal.

Going off the beaten track is part of the adventure. For seasonal produce at its best, seek farmers who sell direct to the public. You find them in farmers' markets, or you can search online for a farmer's website; many do either van deliveries (if local) or mail order. Ask in your health food shop for ideas. Small farmers don't have big budgets to market their wares so it takes a bit of detective work to find them.

## Farmers' markets

Farmers' markets are regulated; stallholders have to be local (within about a 50-mile radius) food producers. As a result of proximity, vegetables arrive vital, not chilled by long days of transportation; indeed most likely picked that morning. Knowing the stallholder is also the vegetable grower adds a new dimension to shopping. You feel more connected to food when it has a story.

## Seasonal organic food and price

Studies show that buying seasonal veg from a farmer's market or organic box delivery (see box below) is cheaper than in a supermarket because there is no middleman to pay. TV chef, Jamie Oliver, uses seasonal organic vegetables in his restaurants. When I asked why, he said: "Good organic food is always healthier for you – it's food with a sparkle. The way things are grown affect their taste. It's not a posh cheffy thing – organic is proper stuff done the old-fashioned way, the right way to work with nature."

Box-clever: Get a veg box delivered to your home, school or office. Choose a scheme to suit you. Some bigger ones offer local and out-of-season imports so there's a wider choice. A small local farmer might only sell home-grown produce but it's seasonal and freshly picked. You can usually choose the size of box to suit your lifestyle, veto a veg and cancel at any point. Search online for 'veg boxes' or ask in a health/whole food shop.

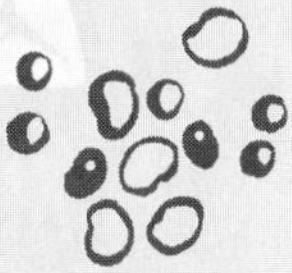

# Growing Peas & Beans

• • •

The stars of this show are peas and beans. Popular around the world since ancient times, they are easily grown and highly nutritious.

## Good for seeds, good for us

Peas and beans are seeds, the plant's future offspring. When they are fully grown, the plant's pods split spilling seeds to the soil where they lie dormant until environmental conditions trigger the process of germination. The food reserves stored within the seeds to support this process are also good for us when we eat them.

Packed with protein, vitamins and minerals, peas and beans are nutritional power-houses. Big yet compact, their plentiful food stores are low-fat yet high-energy. They quieten sugar-levels because of their high levels of fibre, the soluble sort that gently coats the gut with gel and is slow-acting. They also rank in the top 20 for their amazing amounts of cancer-busting antioxidants.

Fresh peas and beans cannot be stored over winter like carrots and onions but they do preserve well. If you can't buy fresh, choose frozen (rather than canned) peas and beans. However dried beans that have already been cooked and then canned are store-cupboard staples and an excellent source of fibre and other nutrients. Uncooked dried beans are preferable, as they are cheaper and more nutritious but that's another story. Our concerns here are fresh peas and beans.

When peas and beans are young and tender, we can eat them whole, pod and seed. For instance, mangetout or French beans are picked before they ripen. Green beans are bred to stay unripe, or green, for longer.

Pea and bean seeds are large, robust and easy-to-handle and produce vigorous seedlings and plants – perfect for beginner gardeners. With their ability to grow upwards, peas and beans make the most of a small space, providing edible beauty with their elegant flowers on long green twining stems.

Peas and beans look different but belong to the same tribe, the legume family. Legumes play a vital role in organic growing because they capture nitrogen from the air and store it in the soil. No need for costly nitrogen fertiliser when you can grow solar-powered legumes to nourish your soil.

## Growing runner beans for beginners

This mini-guide shows you how to grow runner beans in containers outdoors. We suggest you aim for six plants to feed a family of four through the summer months, weather permitting. Runner beans are best for beginners because they are the hardiest member of the legume family, and give the biggest harvest of beans.

You need a patch of ground in a sunny spot to put the three containers on. Three or four canes are stuck in the ground around each container in a wigwam-shape to support the plants. If no ground is available for the sticks, use a wall trellis, fence or screen. Site the containers near the kitchen if possible to keep an eye on your plants and easily water them.

## Timing and biology

You sow the seeds indoors in spring and, by summer, your grown-up plants are outdoors and producing flowers then beans. The more you pick, the more beans your plant will produce. It's biology: the plant's aim is to reproduce – produce seed – before it dies. Picking a bean interrupts the reproduction cycle; tricks the plant into thinking it has not given enough seed. So the plant redoubles its breeding efforts, making more flowers to become beans. Runner bean plants can produce edible beans from June until the first frost of autumn kills them, or the plants run out of steam, whichever comes first. This is generally around the autumn equinox, mid-September.

## Cost-cutting

Don't invest huge sums of money in growing. Your care and attention is what counts.

- Use empty toilet roll cores for sowing. Each cardboard core filled with compost will be a home for a runner bean seed for a good few weeks. Toilet roll cores work well because excess water can evaporate through the cardboard, which prevents over-watering – a common mistake. Start collecting toilet roll cores as soon as you read this. You need 12 for sowing seeds indoors in April.

- Find some containers for your plants that can hold about 10 litres of compost. A 10 litre container is the size of a large bucket and if you are able to make 1cm diameter drainage holes in the bottom, buckets are ideal. Climbing plants are unstable in windy weather so don't skimp on the container size, heavy containers stay upright in rough conditions.

  Another cheap alternative is an empty coffee bean sack (from a coffee bar).

- For cheap compost, buy growbags from a garden centre or hardware shop. If you choose the organic version you will be helping to preserve a peat bog habitat somewhere. Split the bags open, mix the contents with some garden soil that has had the lumps crushed and the large stones picked out, and empty the mixture into your buckets or containers. The added soil will improve the retention of water and nutrients, and provide some ballast to help the plant stay upright when it is windy.

## Sowing seeds

Generally sow your seeds towards the end of April. There is no benefit in sowing earlier as you will end up with leggy seedlings if kept too long indoors. Generally, start sowing at the end of April if you live in the south, while northerners wait till early May. You are aiming to get your seedlings living permanently outdoors on their tray in time for the warm days of late-May.

## List for sowing seeds

Get ready for sowing your seeds indoors by collecting everything you need:

- 12 toilet-roll cores;
- A seed tray to hold them or a tray with drainage holes. Drainage holes are vital because you don't want your rolls standing in a puddle that will prevent their canny ability to let water evaporate through the cardboard. Seed trays are cheap, the right size and reusable for years;
- A packet of runner bean seeds from a garden centre, hardware store or online supplier; and
- 50 litres of organic potting compost from a growbag. You will use a little for sowing in the cardboard cores, and the rest for the big containers.

## Sowing 'recipe'

We are aiming for six plants but starting with 12 seeds. Not all will survive – it's a tough world.

1. Pre-soak your 12 bean seeds to speed up germination, (when the seed comes to life). Cover them in cold water and soak the seeds for eight hours – no more.
2. Place the 12 soaked seeds between several layers of damp kitchen towel in a large-enough dish. The seeds should swell to nearly twice their original size within two to five days.
3. Put the dish in a plastic bag, fold the open end under the dish and keep at a steady 20 degrees – your kitchen is warm enough, or a heated airing cupboard.
4. Within five days to a week, each seed should produce a root. Before the emerging root has reached 1cm long, the seed is ready to be sown in the toilet roll core. Have your 12 empty cores ready on a tray with drainage holes.

5. Take one cardboard core in the palm of your hand. With your other hand, take a fistful of compost, crumbling it into the core until it is two-thirds full.

6. Gently place the soaked seed into the compost, root down, one seed in each tube. Its roots need to be about 3cm beneath the compost, but no deeper, so the seed does not have to grow too far to reach the light. Now add more compost to cover the seed (like pulling the curtains at night), gently pressing the compost to bed down the seed.

7. If everything has gone according to plan, the compost should stay in the core when you place it back on its tray. Continue until you have 12 tubes, ends-up, each with a seed buried in a nutritious environment. The tubes get watered and soggy so lodge them securely in the tray. Keep the tray as near as possible to natural light, ideally a window sill. For now they are staying indoors.

## Looking after your seeds indoors

The roots of the baby seedlings descend seeking water and food, while the stems grow up towards the light. After about two weeks you should see the first shoots emerging. Your main concern is keeping the compost in the cardboard tubes moist but not waterlogged. There is no need to add more nutrients.

Your parenting skills are developing awareness of temperature and light on behalf of your young charges. Your aim is to have your emerging seedlings outside as soon as possible for bursts of the real world of wind, rain and sun. Start getting them used to being outdoors about mid-May (or end of May for the north of the UK). Move the tray outside to a sheltered place for a few hours of sun but always bring it in at night. It's rather like giving a baby in a pram some fresh air every day.

## The last frost of spring

Eventually you want that tray outdoors all night. But when will it be warm enough for your baby seedlings? Low-night temperatures slow-down the plant's metabolism so don't put them outside too early. You need to wait until the risk of a frosty night has passed – the end of May for the south, or mid-June for the north.

A plant needs an equable temperature to thrive; that means warm nights as well as days to make your plants feel comfortable enough to flower – an average of 16 degrees over a period of 24 hours for runner beans. It generally does not get too hot in the UK but it can get too cold and that's what you have to watch out for. Ask a neighbour for local advice about the last frost, if unsure.

### Shopping list for planting outdoors

- 3 x builder's buckets or other suitable containers big enough for 10 litres of compost each. You need to make 1cm diameter drainage holes in the base of your containers if they don't already have them;
- One packet of blood, fish and bone, or a general purpose slow-release fertiliser suitable for vegetarians/vegans, to add to the container's compost three weeks after planting out your seedlings (see Food on p22);
- Extract of seaweed in liquid form. Once diluted with water, it is a weekly nutrient-boost to spray on the bean's leaves (see Food on p22);
- Two plastic sprayers, one for the nutrient-boost, the other to make a simple anti-pest spray using washing-up liquid (see Organic methods of dealing with pests on p23);
- 12m x 3m long bamboo canes;
- String or soft wire to tie the canes; and
- Self-watering device (optional).

## Time to plant outdoors

The tray is a temporary billet. Once the seedling has produced a pair of leaves it is ready to be planted outdoors in its next and final home.

Transplanting is a gentle operation so take it slowly.

1. Fill the three containers with compost emptied from the organic grow bags;
2. Scoop out a hole for the toilet roll core containing its seedling;
3. Water the seedling in its tube;
4. Handling it gently, place the seedling in its core, leaves upwards, in its new home in the big container;
5. Replace the compost around the core without disturbing the seedling's roots too much;
6. Your seedling should be deep enough in its new home so that the lowest leaves are on the surface of the compost then firm the soil around the seedling to gently bed it in.

Choose the six strongest-looking seedlings – this is called 'pricking out' – and discard the weaker ones. You may find that not all 12 seeds have survived anyway. The most vigorous seedlings will make the most robust plants.

## Caring for your growing plant – food, water and support

Once your young plants are bedded in their containers, temperature is no longer an issue. Your focus shifts to the soil. The soil gives the plant food and water and it's your job to make sure it has enough of both. Due to restricted space in containers, you have to water well and feed well. Here's how:

## Water

It's easy to have good watering intentions and as easy to forget them, then make up for neglect with a water-binge. Watering – either over or under – is probably the biggest cause of failure with container-growing. As with the cardboard tubes, the compost in the container has to be moist but not waterlogged.

Timing can be a problem. The main cropping period (when the beans are ready to be picked) starts in August – which usually coincides with people being away on holiday. Luckily there are some cheap and ingenious contraptions available from hardware shops, garden centres and online. Self-watering devices usually consist of a plastic bag or small tank to hold water, some sort of dripper which goes into the container's soil and some flexible tubing to join the two. You can also get devices that are fixed to an empty mineral water bottle (then filled with water). The bag, tank or bottle is raised above the surface of the soil. The height difference can be adjusted to vary the application rate. This system is really useful if you are the sort of person who forgets to water plants.

You can also make your own watering-device with a plastic bottle. Search on the internet or visit **http://tinyurl.com/bbuvp6**

## Food

Your growing beans will need extra food because they are growing in containers. Normally runner bean plants can root about six feet in every direction, gathering nutrients from the soil. In containers, their roots can only grow so far so they need some extra help from you.

Use a fertiliser approved for organic gardening because of its slow-release action. Three weeks after planting the seedlings in their grown-up homes, add dry organic nutrients, such as blood, fish and bone, or any other slow-release general-purpose fertiliser suitable for vegetarians/vegans. Use about 50g in total or two tablespoons per container. Mix this into the top 3cm of soil in each container. And do wash your hands and any kitchen utensils you use afterwards. Repeat four weeks later.

Once your plants are producing plentiful leaves, give them a weekly nutrient-boosting feed. Every week spray their leaves with liquid seaweed feed that has been diluted with water. Apart from providing basic plant-nutrients, foliar feeds provide the plants with lots of other useful nutrients: for example they can help stimulate the plant's defence mechanism against pests and disease. The most effective foliar feeds, whether organically approved or not, come from organic (once-living) sources such as seaweed. Dilute with water, according to the instructions on the packet.

Chase Organics specialises in extract of seaweed – see the mini-appendix at the end of this chapter.

## Organic methods of dealing with pests

Collars cut from large mineral water bottles placed around the base of the plant usually take care of slugs. Once the plants are about 20cm tall, they do not suffer from these pests.

If aphids (greenfly) attack your beans, spray your plants with soapy water. Squirt a couple of drops of washing-up liquid in enough water to make it foamy, and fill a hand-spray. The soapiness disrupts the aphid's waxy skin. Sometimes the force of the water is enough to dislodge the tiny pests.

What are pests to you is food for insects such as ladybirds. Soon natural systems will kick-in to protect your plants as intrepid insect-hunters come looking for food. Hungry for meat such as aphids and other bugs, they will fly far for their food, right up to a high-rise balcony.

Wasps are good news in early summer when they are from a young colony and bug-hunting so leave them alone to do their thing. By late summer they are more interested in a sugary-fruity diet, and then become a nuisance.

## Take note

Keep notes of when and how your seedlings and crops perform. Don't forget to date the entries. Your notes will be useful for the following year.

## Support

A runner bean plant is heavy when carrying a crop. Unstable, it behaves rather like a sail in windy conditions. Without good support and suitable ballast, it can blow over so make sure it is well-supported.

The best support is a wigwam structure of three or four 3m-long bamboo canes pushed into the ground around each container. You tie the tops together with garden twine or soft wire. The plants will naturally twine round the canes but do help them curl round the sticks if necessary. Remember that they twine in a clockwise direction in the northern hemisphere.

If the outdoor space is paved, so no ground is available to stick the canes into, use a wall-mounted wooden trellis or screen. The plants will need a bit more training and tying-in as they grow but will be both secure and decorative.

From now on, training, watering and feeding are the only tasks required until picking starts. The first flowers should appear at the end of June. They will produce their first pods by about mid-July. Feel free to pick them early to try them at different stages to see how they taste. You can't harm the plant – the opposite. As we have said, picking the beans encourages the plant to produce more.

So pick and enjoy!

### Useful suppliers

**Organic gardening catalogue**
**Tel. 0845 130 1304**
**http://www.organiccatalog.com/catalog/**

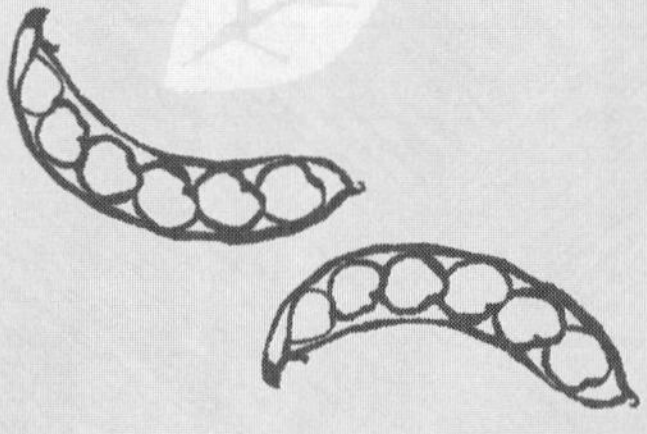

# Recipes

(to serve 4 unless otherwise stated)

by Patricia Harbottle

# Soups & Starters

# Cream of broad bean soup

This velvety soup has the advantage of being a good way to use beans that may be past their youth. However, it really comes into its own with young beans.

**700g (1½lbs) podded fresh or frozen beans**
**40g (1½oz) butter**
**1 tablespoon sunflower oil**
**1 medium skinned and roughly chopped onion**
**2 small peeled and roughly chopped parsnips**
**380ml (13fl oz) light chicken or vegetable stock**
**Bouquet garni**
**150ml (5fl oz) crème fraîche**
**Salt and freshly ground black pepper**
**Sugar if needed**
**Garnish – thin-cut streaky bacon, crisply fried and crumbled**

Heat a large pan of water until boiling and pour in the beans. Cook gently until nearly tender, about 4–5 minutes. Drain, reserving the cooking water. Remove the skins from the beans. This is very quick, providing you don't overcook the beans.

Heat the butter and oil in a large saucepan and add the onion and parsnips. Cover and sweat the vegetables for about 10 minutes. Add the skinned beans, stock and bouquet garni. Cook gently for about 20 minutes until the vegetables are very soft. Allow to cool slightly, pour into a liquidiser or food processor and whizz until you have a thick, smooth puree.

Add a little of the cooking water to the crème fraîche and stir until smooth. Add this to the puree and mix well. Use the cooking water to thin the puree to the desired consistency. Season to taste with salt and freshly ground black pepper. You may need to add a little sugar if the beans are mature. Heat the soup gently but do not boil. Serve in warmed bowls, garnished with the crumbled bacon.

# Bean and herb chowder

1 medium chopped onion
1 thinly sliced leek
2 diced stalks of celery
50g (2oz) butter
100g (3½oz) fresh shelled cannellini beans
150g (5oz) peeled and diced waxy potatoes
Bouquet garni
400ml (14fl oz) light stock
100g (3½oz) diagonally cut runner or helda beans
100g (3½oz) French beans cut into bite-sized pieces
25g (1oz) plain flour
450-600ml (¾ – 1pint) milk
Salt and freshly ground black pepper
Double cream (optional)

Fry the onion, leek and celery over a low heat in half the butter for 15 minutes, stirring frequently. Add the cannellini beans, the potatoes, bouquet garni and the stock and cook for a further 15 minutes. Add all the other beans and cook for another 15 minutes until the vegetables are tender.

In the meantime, use the rest of the butter, the flour and most of the milk to make a fairly thick white sauce. When the beans are cooked, pour a little of the stock into the white sauce to thin it a bit and then tip the sauce onto the vegetables and stir well. Season with salt and freshly ground black pepper to taste. Now it is up to you how rib-sticking you want the soup to be. Thin the mixture to the required consistency. You can enrich this soup by adding some cream at the end.

# Spiced pea soup

2 tablespoons sunflower oil
1 teaspoon ground coriander
2 teaspoons ground cumin
1 large, peeled roughly chopped onion
2 peeled, roughly chopped cloves of garlic
2½cm (1 inch) knob of peeled and grated fresh ginger
1 roughly chopped, deseeded green chilli
600ml (1 pint) chicken stock
500g (18oz) fresh or frozen peas
150ml (5fl oz) single cream
Salt
Chopped coriander leaves to garnish

Heat the oil in a large pan and stir-fry the coriander and cumin for a minute. Add the onion, garlic, ginger and chilli. Cover the pan and sweat the vegetables for 10 minutes over a low heat.

Add the stock and bring to the boil before adding the peas. Simmer gently for 15 minutes. Cool slightly and pour into a blender or food processor and whizz until smooth. Put the soup back in the pan and stir in the cream. Season with salt to taste. Reheat without boiling. Serve in bowls and garnish with chopped fresh coriander leaves.

# Pea and pak choy soup

**40g (1½oz) dried shitaki mushrooms**
**1.2 litres (2 pints) of duck or chicken stock**
**1 thinly sliced stalk of lemon grass**
**2½cm (1 inch) knob of peeled and chopped fresh ginger root**
**2 peeled and chopped cloves of garlic**
**1 level tablespoon miso paste (optional)**
**1–2 deseeded, sliced small red Thai chillies**
**250g (9oz) fresh or frozen peas**
**120g (4oz) washed and chopped pak choy**
**Salt if not using the miso paste, and freshly ground black pepper**

To rehydrate the mushrooms, soak in warm water for at least 30 minutes. Drain, retaining the soaking water and slice them thinly.

Pour the stock into a large saucepan together with the mushroom water. Bring to the boil and add the lemon grass, ginger and garlic. Simmer for 15–20 minutes. Strain into a clean pan and discard the vegetables.

If using the miso paste, put a ladleful of hot stock in a small bowl and melt the paste in it. Put the pan back on the heat, add the chillis and mushrooms and simmer for 10 minutes. Add the peas, bring the pan back to boiling point, and slide in the pak choy. Simmer for no more than 2 minutes. Stir in the melted miso paste, adjust the seasoning and serve immediately.

# Pea and prawn roulade

**80g (3oz) white breadcrumbs**
**4 large eggs, separated**
**120g (4oz) pea puree (recipe page 85)**
**150ml (5fl oz) full fat milk**
**Salt and pepper**

**For the filling:**

**2 tablespoons crème fraîche**
**175g (6oz) any mild, soft creamy cheese**
**Lemon juice**
**120g (4oz) defrosted or fresh, roughly chopped cooked prawns**
**A few drops of angostura bitters (optional)**
**A little salt and freshly ground black pepper**

Grease the base and sides of a 36 x 26cm Swiss roll tin and line with non-stick baking parchment. Grease the parchment too.

Make the filling by stirring the crème fraîche into the soft cheese. Stir in a squeeze of lemon juice to get a spreadable mixture. Add the prawns, angostura bitters if using and seasoning and combine thoroughly.

Place the breadcrumbs into the bottom of a large mixing bowl, making a well in the centre. Put the egg yolks into this together with the pea puree. Add the milk, salt and pepper. Stir the mixture until well blended.

In a separate bowl, beat the egg whites until they form soft peaks. Fold 1/3 of them gently into the breadcrumb mixture, then fold in the rest. Pour into the Swiss roll tin, and spread the mixture evenly, making sure you get right into the corners. Bake in a preheated oven at 200°C (180°C if using a fan oven) or Gas Mark 6 for 10–15 minutes until risen and just firm.

Remove from the oven and cover with a damp tea towel to stop the roulade from drying out and cracking. Leave to cool. Run a thin knife or spatula round the edge of the tin to make sure the roulade is loosened, then turn out onto another sheet of baking parchment. Peel off the baking parchment and spread the filling evenly over the surface, leaving about 2½cms (1 inch) round the edges. With the long side of the roulade towards you, take hold of the parchment and firmly roll into a long sausage, like a Swiss roll. Serve, cut into slices, garnished with lemon wedges and watercress.

# Oeufs en cocotte with green beans

**8 rashers of thin sliced smoked streaky bacon**
**50g (2oz) fine French beans**
**4 large eggs**
**4 tablespoons crème fraîche**
**Freshly ground black pepper**

You need 4 well-greased ramekin dishes with minimum internal measurements of 9cm (3½ inches) diameter and 4cm (1½ inches) depth.

Cut the bacon rashers into approximately 2cm (¾ inch) squares. Stir-fry in a small frying pan until just starting to brown at the edges. Set aside to cool.

Wash and trim the beans and boil in a pan of salted water until "al dente". Drain, reserving the water for a useful stock. Plunge the beans into cold water to cool and stop them cooking. Slice across into small pieces.

Divide the chopped beans equally between the 4 ramekins and sprinkle the bacon on top of them. Crack an egg on top of each dish. Top them with a tablespoon of crème fraîche, covering the egg as much as possible. Season with freshly ground black pepper.

Put the ramekins into a roasting tin. Pour enough boiling water round them to come half way up the sides of the dishes. Bake in a preheated oven at 180°C (160°C if using a fan oven) or Gas Mark 4 for 10–15 minutes until the white is set and the yolk still runny. You can keep these eggs warm in their hot bath for a short length of time before serving, in which case leave them slightly undercooked so they remain soft.

# Pea soufflé

2 tablespoons butter
2 tablespoons plain flour
250ml (9fl oz) hot milk
2 tablespoons freshly grated gruyere cheese
2 tablespoons freshly grated parmesan cheese
2 eggs, separated
250g (9oz) pea puree (recipe page 85)
Salt and pepper

Melt the butter in a pan and stir in the flour. Cook, stirring for a minute or two, then gradually add the hot milk to make a white sauce. Cook for 3–5 minutes, stirring all the time. Take the pan off the heat and stir in the cheeses and egg yolks. Mix in the pea puree and season with salt and freshly ground pepper.

Beat the egg whites with a pinch of salt until quite stiff and gently fold half of them into the contents of the pan. Fold in the remaining egg whites. Pour the mixture into a well-buttered soufflé dish and bake at 150°C (130°C if using a fan oven) or Gas Mark 2 for about 30 minutes until risen and golden brown on top. Serve immediately.

# Pea custards with tomato sauce

175g (6oz) pea puree (recipe page 85)
40g (1½oz) finely chopped shallot
10g (½oz) butter
2 eggs and 2 egg yolks
Salt and freshly ground black pepper
A pinch of mace
100ml (3½fl oz) milk
200ml (7fl oz) crème fraîche
50g (2oz) freshly grated parmesan cheese

**For the sauce:**

1 tablespoon olive oil
1 finely chopped small onion
1 finely chopped clove of garlic
225g (8oz) peeled, cored, deseeded and chopped tomato
Salt, freshly ground black pepper and a pinch of sugar

Make the sauce by heating the oil in a small pan and adding the onion and garlic. Fry gently for at least 10 minutes until soft but not browned. Add the chopped tomatoes and seasonings and simmer for 5 minutes until the juice runs out. Turn up the heat and cook fast for 10 minutes until some of the liquid has evaporated. The shorter the cooking time, the fresher the sauce tastes.

Make a batch of pea puree, leaving out the lemon juice. (You can always add lemon juice to what's left over before freezing or using in another dish).

Gently fry the finely chopped shallot in the butter until soft and add to the puree. Put the mixture through the fine disc of a vegetable mill.

Whisk the eggs and yolks together and season with salt, freshly ground black pepper and mace.

Whisk the milk into the crème fraîche and add to the egg mixture together with the cheese. Stir the liquids into the pea puree being careful to mix it well, then pour into 4 buttered ramekin dishes. The mixture should come nearly to the rims. Put the ramekins into a baking dish and fill the dish with hot water to come half way up the sides of the dishes. Bake in the oven at 180°C (160°C if using a fan oven) or Gas Mark 4 for 30 minutes, until firm to the touch.

To serve, run a knife round the custards to loosen them and turn out onto 4 warmed plates. Add a spoonful of tomato sauce to each plate. Crusty bread goes well with this.

# Michelle's duck and pea terrine

Serves 6.

**1 duck**
**1 peeled and roughly chopped onion**
**1 roughly chopped large carrot**
**1 or 2 sticks roughly chopped celery**
**A few mushroom stalks**
**A handful of parsley**
**½ teaspoon salt**
**1 teaspoon black peppercorns**
**150ml (5fl oz) red wine**
**450g (1lb) fresh or frozen peas**
**50g (2oz) butter**
**5cm (2 inch) piece peeled, thinly sliced fresh ginger**
**4–6 large, thinly sliced cloves of garlic**
**Salt**

Put the duck into a large pan with the onion, carrot, celery, mushroom stalks, parsley, salt and peppercorns. Add the red wine and top up with water to cover the bird. Bring slowly to the boil and simmer for 40 minutes. Add the peas and continue to cook for a further 15 minutes. Lift the duck out onto a carving plate and cool until you can handle it. Remove the skin and slice the duck breast. Set aside.

Remove the rest of the meat from the bird, discarding any skin and fat, and cut up the larger bits.

Drain the stock through a colander into a large bowl. Discard the carrot, celery and some of the peppercorns, unless you like your terrine to be quite peppery.

Meanwhile, melt the butter in a frying pan, add the ginger and garlic and fry very gently until they are just starting to colour.

Put the duck pieces into a processor together with the peas, ginger and garlic and puree them all thoroughly. Season to taste with salt.

Take a medium-sized loaf tin and line the bottom with greaseproof paper or baking parchment. Spread half the puree over the bottom of the tin. Arrange the carved duck breast on top and cover with the rest of the puree, spreading it evenly.

Chill well before running a knife round the sides of the tin and gently turning the terrine out onto a serving plate. Slice across and serve with toast or salad.

# Broad bean pate

**450g (1lb) podded, elderly broad beans**
**1 clove of garlic**
**1 teaspoon Magic Masala**
**The juice of 1 lime**
**2 tablespoons extra virgin olive oil**
**Salt and freshly ground black pepper**

Boil the beans for about 15 minutes until tender, then pop them out of their skins.

Put the beans with the rest of the ingredients, apart from the salt and pepper, into a food processor and whizz until you have the desired consistency. You may want to leave it rough or go on until it is smooth. Season to taste with salt and freshly ground black pepper.

Magic Masala is a product that I can highly recommend. You can buy it and other spices, from the New York Delhi Company, on the internet at www.newyorkdelhi.com. Failing that, you could make a homemade version by using a mixture of powdered mace, ginger, fenugreek, clove, cinnamon, coriander, cumin, turmeric, cardamom and chilli. The quantities of each spice depends rather on your taste, but use equal quantities of the ones you like and lesser of the others until you get the right mix.

# French beans wrapped in parma ham

This takes 10 minutes at the most and is brilliant for a quick starter.

**12 trimmed French beans per person**
**3 drops Tabasco sauce**
**50g (2oz) curd cheese**
**A little milk or cream**
**4 slices parma or other air-dried ham**
**Salad leaves or watercress to garnish**

Steam the French beans until "al dente". Cool in cold water and drain well.

Mix the Tabasco sauce into the curd cheese and thin very slightly with milk or cream to make it easier to spread.

Spread a thin layer of the cheese over the surface of the ham slices and arrange the beans across the slice in a row, leaving some space at each end of the slice. Now roll up the slices into a tube. Put onto four plates and garnish with the leaves.

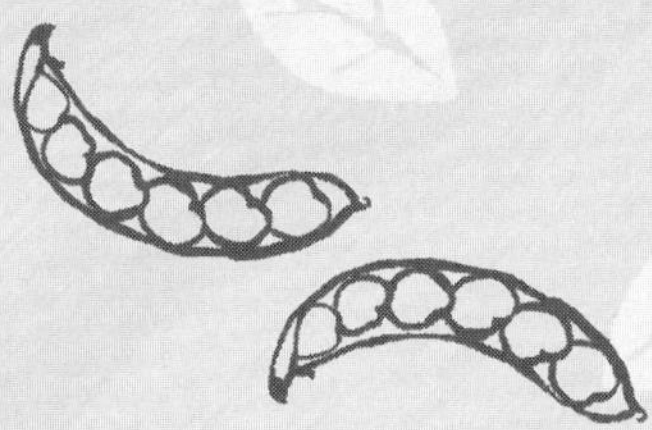

# Main Dishes

# Salmon and runner bean bake

**350g (12oz) runner beans**
**40g (1½oz) butter plus extra for the topping**
**40g (1½oz) plain flour**
**½ teaspoon English mustard powder**
**280ml (10fl oz) light chicken or fish stock**
**250ml (9fl oz) milk**
**A handful of chopped fresh parsley leaves**
**50g (2oz) grated mature cheddar cheese**
**450g (1lb) skinned, thick salmon fillet, cut into large cubes**
**Fresh breadcrumbs**

Boil or steam the runner beans until nearly tender (5–10 minutes). If you steam them they will retain more flavour. Put them into a bath of cold water to stop them cooking further and then drain.

Make a bechamel sauce with the butter, flour, mustard powder, stock and milk. You need a sauce that just runs off the spoon, so add a little more milk if necessary. Stir in the parsley and cheese and cook until the cheese melts. Take the sauce off the heat and fold in the fish while the sauce is still hot.

Grease a large pie dish and spoon half the beans into it. Add a layer of fish mixture, the rest of the beans and then the rest of the fish. Top with a good layer of breadcrumbs and dot with butter. Bake near the top of the oven preheated to 200°C (180°C if using a fan oven) or Gas Mark 6 for 20 minutes.

# Braised beef, beans and preserved lemon

**120g (4oz) lardons or cubed pancetta**
**16 baby onions**
**A little beef dripping**
**4 braising steaks about 200g (7oz) each**
**2-3 large crushed cloves of garlic**
**200ml (7fl oz) good red wine**
**200ml (7fl oz) beef, chicken or bean stock**
**Bouquet garni**
**Freshly ground black pepper**
**80g (3oz) helda or runner beans**
**80g (3oz) French beans**
**10g (½oz) softened butter**
**10g (½oz) plain flour**
**2 tablespoons preserved lemon segments or slices**

In a non-stick pan, fry the lardons for 5 minutes until taking on colour. Set aside and fry the onions in the fat from the bacon to brown them slightly. Set aside.

Heat the dripping in the pan over a high heat. Sear the steaks for one minute on each side to seal. Put the meat, bacon and onions in a casserole.

Add the garlic, wine, stock, bouquet garni and pepper. (Do not add any salt as the bacon is salty and the lemons are preserved in salt). Bring gently to the boil, cover and put into an oven at 150°C (130°C if using a fan oven) or Gas Mark 2 for 1 hour 15 minutes. Add the beans and cook for a further 30 minutes until everything is tender.

Drain the liquid out of the casserole into a pan. Mix the butter and flour together to make a paste. Put the pan on a medium heat and whisk in the butter and flour mixture a little at a time until it has thickened the liquid to the desired consistency. Pour the sauce back into the casserole and stir in the drained, preserved lemon. Cover and put the casserole back in the oven to simmer for 15 minutes to blend the flavours.

# Casserole of pork and mixed beans

**4 rashers diced thick-cut smoked streaky bacon**
**1 tablespoon chicken fat or vegetable oil**
**16 button onions**
**450g (1lb) lean stewing pork**
**250ml (9fl oz) medium dry white wine**
**150ml (5fl oz) water or stock**
**1 bay leaf**
**1 sprig of thyme**
**12 whole unpeeled small new potatoes**
**Salt and pepper**
**350g (12oz) of any mixture of runner, broad, French, helda, fresh borlotti or soya beans**
**1 tablespoon softened butter**
**1 tablespoon plain flour**
**Chopped parsley to garnish**

Dry fry the bacon in a frying pan until it is nice and brown and has given off its fat. Remove to a large casserole, leaving the fat behind. Add the chicken fat or oil to the frying pan and fry the button onions until they start to take on colour. Place in the casserole. Turn the heat to high and fry the pork in small batches until brown and combine with the other ingredients in the casserole.

Pour the wine into the frying pan and scrape up all the brown bits, then pour the wine and water or stock over the meat in the casserole. Add the herbs and potatoes and season to taste with salt and pepper. Cook the casserole in an oven at 180°C (160°C if using a fan oven) or Gas Mark 4 for an hour, stirring every 15 minutes. While it is cooking, steam your chosen beans until almost tender. It is best to steam each type of bean separately.

Remove the meat and potatoes to a bowl and keep warm while you thicken the sauce.

Mix the softened butter and flour together to make a beurre manié. Put the casserole on the hob and bring the juices to the boil. Gradually whisk in small spoonfuls of the beurre manié to thicken and cook the sauce, then put the meat and potatoes back and add the beans to the pot. Turn the oven heat down to 150°C (130°C if using a fan oven) or Gas Mark 2 and cook the casserole until everything is tender. Check the seasoning before serving sprinkled with the chopped parsley.

# Braised pigeon with fresh borlotti beans

**Sunflower oil**
**120g (4oz) chopped thick bacon rashers or lardons**
**4 oven-ready wood pigeon**
**16 button onions**
**2 finely chopped cloves of garlic**
**300g (10oz) peeled, cubed parsnips**
**400g (14oz) fresh borlotti beans**
**500ml (17fl oz) stock**
**2 sprigs of sage**
**Salt and freshly ground black pepper**

Stir-fry the bacon in a trace of sunflower oil until turning brown. Remove to a deep casserole big enough to hold the pigeons.

Brown the pigeons all over in the bacon fat and add to the casserole. Next, brown the onions in the fat, adding the garlic after a few minutes. Be careful not to burn the garlic. Scrape the onions and garlic into the casserole.

Brown the parsnips for about 5 minutes, adding a little more oil if necessary, and put them in the casserole together with the borlotti beans and stock. Put the sprigs of sage on top of the birds, cover the casserole with a tight fitting lid and braise in a moderate oven for about an hour until the birds are cooked. Season with salt and black pepper and leave to rest for 5 minutes before serving.

# Duck, pea and orange pie

**For the duck stock and fat:**

5–6 medium duck legs
1 large roughly chopped carrot
1 peeled and roughly chopped medium onion
2 sticks roughly chopped celery

**For the pie:**

2 large oranges
2 tablespoons duck fat
1 finely chopped medium onion
About 250ml (9fl oz) duck stock
I tablespoon potato flour or cornflour
Salt and freshly ground black pepper
200g (7oz) fresh or frozen peas
Shortcrust or puff pastry to cover

Heat the oven to 220°C (200°C if using a fan oven) or Gas Mark 7. Skin the duck legs. Don't bother to remove the skin from the bottom bone, where there is no meat. Put the skins into a roasting tin and put in the oven for about 20 minutes to render down and obtain the lovely duck fat that runs out of them. Be careful not to burn them.

Put the legs into a large pan with the roughly chopped vegetables. Cover with water and simmer for 30 minutes. Cool. Take the meat off the bones and cut into bite-sized pieces. Put the duck bones back in the pan and reduce the stock to about ½ pint.

Finely grate the zest from one orange. Cut away the peel and pith from both the oranges. Cut the segments out, leaving the membrane. Catch the escaping juice in a bowl and squeeze the bundle of membranes in your hand to get the last of the juice.

Use 2 tablespoons of the duck fat to fry the finely chopped onion for about 10 minutes to soften. (Save the rest of the duck fat to roast lovely crispy potatoes.) Add the strained stock. Stir the potato or cornflour into the orange juice and add to the pan. Heat, stirring until the sauce thickens. Season to taste with salt and pepper.

Cut the orange segments in half if they are large. Add the duck meat, orange segments and peas to the sauce. Tip into a medium pie dish and top with your choice of pastry. Make one or two steam holes in the pastry, brush with beaten egg. Put the pie in the hot oven for 10 minutes then turn the heat down to 180°C (160°C if using a fan oven) or Gas Mark 4 and bake for 20–30 minutes until the pastry is cooked and golden brown.

# Mild spiced minced lamb and peas

This is very mild with children in mind, but obviously you can make it as spicy as you like.

**2 tablespoons sunflower oil**
**1 large finely chopped onion**
**4 large crushed cloves of garlic**
**450g (1lb) minced lamb**
**1 deseeded, chopped fresh green chilli**
**2½cm (1 inch) piece of peeled, grated fresh ginger root**
**A pinch of cayenne pepper**
**2 teaspoons ground cumin**
**1 teaspoon ground coriander**
**250ml (9fl oz) lamb stock or water and crumbled stock cube**
**200g (7oz) fresh or frozen peas**
**A large handful of chopped, fresh coriander leaves**
**Salt and pepper**
**2 tablespoons plain yoghurt**

Heat the oil in a pan and fry the onion for about 10 minutes until soft and beginning to brown. Add the garlic and stir-fry for 1–2 minutes.

Add the minced lamb in small quantities, stirring and breaking up the lumps. When it is all nice and brown, add the chilli, ginger root, cayenne, cumin and coriander. Cook for a few more minutes before adding the stock. Bring the mixture to the boil and simmer for 30–40 minutes.

Stir in the peas and simmer for a further few minutes to cook them, then stir in the coriander leaves and seasoning. Allow to cool a little and stir in the yoghurt.

You can serve this with plain boiled rice or mashed potato.

# Sugar-snap peas with prawns, mushrooms and lemon rice

**500g (18oz) best quality frozen cooked, peeled prawns**
**300g (10oz) trimmed sugar-snap peas**
**2 tablespoons sunflower oil**
**Thinly sliced white parts of 6 spring onions**
**2½cm (1 inch) knob of peeled and grated fresh ginger**
**2 finely chopped cloves of garlic**
**2–3 deseeded chopped green chillies**
**150g (5oz) quartered button mushrooms**

**For the rice:**

**500g (18oz) long grain rice**
**Grated zest and juice of 1 lemon**
**The juice from the defrosted prawns**

Defrost the prawns naturally. Do not microwave them. Reserve the liquid that runs off them.

Steam the sugar-snap peas for 3 minutes until tender. (They cook very quickly.) Drain and keep warm.

Boil the rice according to the guidelines on the packet, making sure you leave it "al dente". Drain the rice, place in a dish and pour over the juice from the prawns mixed with zest and juice of the lemon. Keep warm.

Meanwhile, stir-fry the spring onion first over a moderate heat for 1–2 minutes, then the ginger, garlic and chillies for a further 2 minutes. Add the mushrooms to the pan and stir-fry for another 3 minutes. Add the sugar-snap peas and prawns and heat through.

Spread the rice into a hot dish and spoon over the prawn mixture, or serve on individual hot plates.

# Pea, bean and anchovy quiche

**80g (3oz) trimmed French beans, cut into 2½cm (1 inch) lengths**
**80g (3oz) fresh or defrosted frozen peas**
**10g (½oz) butter**
**1 small, finely chopped onion**
**2 large eggs**
**250ml (9fl oz) milk**
**60ml (2fl oz) double cream**
**Freshly ground black pepper**
**20cm (8 inch) shortcrust pastry case, baked blind**
**A small tin of anchovy fillets**

Put a small pan of salted water on to boil. When it is bubbling away, add the beans. Boil for about 5 minutes until almost tender then add the peas. Boil for an additional minute. Drain, saving the water to use for stock. Run the cold tap over the vegetables to stop them cooking and leave to dry on a shallow tray, on kitchen paper.

Melt the butter in a small frying pan. Gently fry the onion for 5–10 minutes until soft but not browned. Leave to cool.

Crack the eggs into a bowl and beat with a fork to loosen them. Add the milk and cream and beat again. Season with freshly ground black pepper. Add the onions and butter into the egg mixture and mix well.

Spread the peas and beans evenly in the pastry case. Lay the anchovy fillets like the spokes of a wheel on top and pour over the egg and milk mixture. Bake for approximately 30 minutes until set at 150°C (130°C if using a fan oven) or Gas Mark 2.

Delicious served warm with a salad.

# Summer vegetable pasta

**2 carrots peeled and cut into matchsticks**
**6 spring onions, washed, trimmed and cut into bite-sized lengths**
**120g (4oz) French beans, washed, trimmed and cut into bite-sized lengths**
**120g (4oz) runner beans, washed, trimmed and cut into diamonds**
**120g (4oz) shelled broad beans**
**120g (4oz) shelled peas**
**1 large egg**
**150ml (5fl oz) double cream**
**50g (2oz) grated parmesan cheese**
**225g (8oz) tubular pasta (rigatoni is best)**
**2 tablespoons chopped parsley**

Steam the carrots for about 5 minutes until just starting to soften. Add the spring onions and cook until almost soft. Remove to a warm dish and put the French and runner beans on to steam, cooking them until they too are left with a little crunch. Add them to the carrots. Now cook your peas and broad beans in the same manner. If either of these last two is frozen, it is best to boil them for a minute or two before they join the other vegetables to keep warm.

Beat the egg, cream and cheese until they are well mixed.

If you have any bean or pea stock stored, add this to a large pan of well salted water and bring to the boil. Add the pasta and cook according to the directions on the packet. Drain the pasta and tip in the egg mixture while it is still very hot. Mix well, then add the vegetables and parsley. Serve immediately.

# Bean and pea frittata

Serves 6.

**225g (8oz) French beans**
**225g (8oz) fresh shelled or frozen peas**
**1 tablespoon sunflower oil**
**1 large diced onion**
**Small clove of finely chopped garlic**
**10 eggs**
**3 tablespoons milk**
**2 teaspoons chopped oregano**
**Salt and freshly ground black pepper**

Steam the beans until tender and likewise boil the peas.

Fry the onion and garlic in a large omelette pan. Beat the eggs and milk together lightly, add the vegetables, oregano and seasoning and tip into the omelette pan over a slow heat. Allow the egg to set on the bottom of the pan before easing the frittata away from the edges to let the uncooked egg to get underneath the set part. Continue to do this until most of the uncooked egg has seeped through and cooked.

Have your grill ready on medium heat. Put the frittata under the grill to set and brown the top.

This can be served hot, warm or cold and is great for picnics.

# Chicken, pea and bean stir-fry

1 tablespoon groundnut or sunflower oil
A bunch of spring onions
2 fat, finely chopped cloves of garlic
2½cm (1 inch) knob of fresh finely chopped ginger
500g (18oz) skinned chicken breasts, cut into strips
120g (4oz) trimmed mangetout
120g (4oz) trimmed sugar-snap peas
120g (4oz) trimmed and sliced runner or helda beans
120g (4oz) French beans, cut in 4cm lengths
2 large handfuls of sliced Chinese cabbage (Chinese leaf)
2 large handfuls of beansprouts

**For the marinade:**

2½cm (1 inch) knob of peeled and grated fresh ginger
2 tablespoons groundnut or sunflower oil
2 tablespoons dark soy sauce
Chilli sauce

Mix all the marinade ingredients together, using as much chilli sauce as you think appropriate – anything from half a teaspoon to a tablespoon. Add the chicken strips and allow to marinate for at least 2 hours.

Heat the oil in your wok until it is really hot and add the spring onions, garlic and ginger for 30 seconds before adding the chicken pieces. Stir-fry for 2 minutes then add the peas and beans. Continue stir-frying for a further 3 minutes, then pour in the marinade. Turn the heat to low and simmer until the chicken is cooked and the vegetables are nice and crunchy. Throw in the Chinese cabbage and beansprouts, stir and serve immediately.

# Thai green curry

This recipe and the one that follows come from my wonderful daughter, Sue. She loves to travel and these were collected on her trips abroad.

**For the green curry paste:**

2 teaspoons dried galangal, soaked for 30 mins and chopped
Half a chopped onion
6 chopped cloves of garlic
6 chillies
2 chopped stalks of lemon grass
Bunch of coriander with roots, chopped
2 sliced bay leaves
6 ground black peppercorns
1 ground teaspoon cumin seeds
1 ground teaspoon coriander seeds
Zest of a lime
2½cm (1 inch) knob of peeled fresh ginger
Half a teaspoon salt

Grind all the above ingredients to a smooth paste in a pestle and mortar or a food processor. Transfer to a jar unless using immediately.

**For the curry:**

2 tablespoons sunflower oil
350g (12oz) pork tenderloin (or chicken breast meat)
3 tablespoons curry paste, either made as above or bought
1 tin of coconut milk
3 lime leaves, soaked for 10 minutes and sliced
3 tablespoons fish sauce
2 teaspoons sugar
Juice of a lime
450g (1lb) of French beans, topped, tailed and chopped into
5cm (2 inch) pieces.

Slice the pork or chicken into 1cm (½ inch) thick slices and brown in the sunflower oil in a wide pan. Remove and keep warm.

In the same pan fry the curry paste for a few minutes to release the flavours. Add the coconut milk, lime leaves, fish sauce, sugar and lime juice and simmer until reduced and thickened a bit. While this is happening steam the green beans for a couple of minutes. Add the pork or chicken and the beans to the sauce and simmer all together until the beans are just tender but still green. Serve with lots of rice to soak up the scrummy sauce.

# Taze fasulye (Green bean stew)

The people of Turkey are deservedly renowned for their immense warmth and hospitality. On the first of many visits there by my daughter and her friend Karen, they took to the mountains, travelling by bus from their holiday resort on the south coast. Finding they had a while to wait for their bus to the town of Mugla, they met an elderly chap with twinkly eyes, who took them under his wing and insisted that they go and eat lunch with him and his family. Whenever my daughter cooks this dish, she remembers the kindness of these people who shared their simple lunch with two young women who thereupon fell deeply in love with the country, the people and – of course – the food.

**2 onions, sliced finely**
**2 cloves of garlic, sliced finely**
**100ml (3½fl oz) olive oil**
**1 kilo (2lbs 2oz) fresh runner beans, topped and tailed and cut into pieces if they are very long**
**500g (18oz) fresh tomatoes chopped, or a 400g (14oz) can of chopped tomatoes**
**Salt and black pepper**
**1 teaspoon sugar**
**Hot water**

Fry the onion and garlic very slowly in the oil until just golden. Stir in the beans and coat them thoroughly with the oil. Add the tomatoes, salt, pepper and sugar, and mix well. If the stew looks a little dry add some hot water (if using fresh tomatoes you may require a little more than if you're using canned ones).

Cover and cook for about 20 minutes or until the beans are tender and have absorbed quite a bit of the juice. This can be served hot or at room temperature.

# Cheesy pea and bean pie

**120g (4oz) mangetout**
**120g (4oz) sugar snap peas**
**80g (3oz) helda beans**
**80g (3oz) green beans**
**80g (3oz) runner beans**
**40g (1½oz) butter**
**2 medium sliced young leeks**
**40g (1½oz) plain flour**
**150ml (5fl oz) chicken stock**
**150ml (5fl oz) milk**
**Salt, freshly ground black pepper and ½ teaspoon Dijon mustard**
**50g (2oz) grated mature cheddar cheese**
**Shortcrust or puff pastry to cover a 28cm (11 inch) pie dish**

Steam the mangetout and sugar snaps for 3 minutes. Cut them in half across. Steam the beans for 7 minutes. Cut them into bite-sized pieces.

Heat the butter in a medium sized pan. Sauté the leeks for 5 minutes. Remove from the pan and add the flour to the remaining butter. Cook, stirring for 1–2 minutes and then gradually add the stock and milk, stirring all the time to make a thick sauce. Season with the salt, pepper and Dijon mustard and stir in the cheese. Cook for 2–3 minutes.

Tip the leeks and other vegetables into the pan and stir to coat with the sauce. Put the mixture into a 28cm (11 inch) pie dish. Roll out the pastry and cover the pie with it, sealing the edges. Make a hole in the middle to let the steam escape and decorate with pastry trimmings if desired. Brush the pastry with beaten egg and bake in an oven at 200°C (180°C if using a fan oven) or Gas Mark 6 for 10 minutes. Turn the oven down to 160°C (140°C for a fan oven) or Gas Mark 3 and bake for 30 minutes until the pastry is cooked and golden brown.

# Anna's French beans torta

Anna says that you can eat this dish hot or cold but not straight out of the oven or chilled. She gave it to us when we had lunch with her one day and I asked her if she would give me the recipe. It is special.

**25g (1oz) dried porcini mushrooms**
**250g (9oz) floury potatoes**
**500g (18oz) French beans**
**2 free-range eggs**
**75g (2½oz) freshly grated Parmesan cheese**
**Salt and pepper to taste**
**1 teaspoon chopped fresh marjoram**
**3 tablespoons extra virgin olive oil**
**Dried breadcrumbs**

Put the mushrooms into a bowl and soak in hot water for 30 minutes. Rinse them if they are gritty and pat dry on kitchen paper. Chop them coarsely.

Scrub the potatoes and cook them in their skins in boiling water. Drain and peel them as soon as they are cool enough to handle. Puree them, or rice them if you have a potato ricer. Put them in a large bowl with the porcini.

Top and tail the beans, wash them and cook in boiling water until just tender (5–10 minutes). Drain, dry on kitchen paper, chop and add to the porcini and potatoes.

Lightly beat the eggs with the Parmesan, salt, pepper and marjoram. Stir into the potato mixture. Mix in 1 tablespoon of the olive oil, taste and adjust the seasoning. Grease a 20cm (8 inch) ovenproof baking dish with 1 tablespoon of the remaining oil and sprinkle some dried breadcrumbs all over the inside of the dish, shaking off any excess crumbs. Spoon the vegetable mixture into the dish and spread out evenly. Cover lightly with more dried breadcrumbs and sprinkle with the remaining olive oil. Bake at 180°C (160°C if using a fan oven) or Gas Mark 4 for about an hour until a light golden crust has formed.

# Side Dishes

# Peas with mint, garlic and lemon butter

**25g (1oz) butter**
**2 cloves of crushed new season's fresh garlic**
**1–2 tablepoons lemon juice**
**2 kilos (4lbs 4oz) young garden peas in the pod**
**The chopped leaves from 2 stalks of mint**

Melt the butter in a small pan. Add the garlic and cook very gently for a minute or two, then add the lemon juice. It is a matter of taste but I like this mixture not too lemony.

Shell the peas. Cook and drain them, keeping the water for vegetable stock. Add the mint to the butter mixture and reheat gently before pouring over the peas in a serving bowl.

So simple but utterly delicious!

# Sugar-snap peas with egg and lemon sauce

**600g (1¼lbs) trimmed and stringed (if necessary) sugar-snap peas**
**The yolks of three large eggs**
**30ml (1fl oz) lemon juice**
**Good pinch sugar**
**100ml (3½fl oz) water from cooking the peas**

Cook the sugar-snaps in boiling water until tender, about 3 minutes. Drain and reserve the water.

In a small pan, mix the egg yolks, lemon juice and sugar together and put over a gentle heat. Warm the mixture, gently stirring all the time being very careful not to scramble the egg. Add the hot water a little at a time and stir the sauce well until it thickens and coats the back of the spoon. Pour over the peas and serve. Delicious with fish or chicken.

# Broad beans with cream and herbs

**500g (18oz) shelled young broad beans**
**40g (1½oz) butter**
**1 peeled and finely chopped clove of garlic**
**200ml (7fl oz) crème fraîche**
**50ml (1¾fl oz) double cream**
**A small handful of chopped mixed herbs (nothing too strong – parsley, thyme and chives perhaps)**
**Salt and pepper**

Boil the beans until tender. Drain, saving the cooking water for stock. Refresh in cold water and pop them out of their skins.

Melt the butter in a frying pan and gently fry the garlic for one minute. Mix the crème fraîche and cream together. Add the beans, herbs and creams to the pan, season to taste and let the mixture bubble for a minute before serving.

Great with fish and chicken, or even on toast!

# Mario Antonelli's beans in tomato sauce

This recipe was given to me by an old friend who is half Italian, half Greek. I have adapted it slightly.

**4 tablespoons olive oil**
**1 large chopped onion**
**1 fat clove of garlic, preferably new season**
**2 diced carrots**
**3 diced celery stalks including leaves**
**400g (14oz) can chopped tomatoes**
**1 tablespoon tomato puree**
**Salt, pepper and sugar to taste**
**400g (14oz) runner or helda beans cut across into bite-sized pieces**
**Chopped parsley to garnish**

Heat the oil and sweat the onion and garlic for a good 5 minutes, add the carrot and celery and cook gently until soft but not brown. Add the tomatoes and tomato puree. Season with salt, pepper and a pinch of sugar. Put the lid on the pan and cook gently for 15 minutes until the tomatoes start to break down.

Steam the beans for about 8 minutes until beginning to soften then add them to the sauce to finish cooking. Garnish with parsley and serve hot with grilled meat or white fish, or cold as a salad.

# Runner beans au gratin

**450g (1lb) runner beans**
**180ml (6fl oz) half fat crème fraîche**
**180ml (6fl oz) double cream**
**Salt, pepper and a scraping of nutmeg**
**40g (1½oz) freshly grated gruyere cheese**
**20g (¾oz) freshly grated parmesan cheese**

Wash the beans, string them and cut them across diagonally into bite-sized diamond pieces. Steam for 8–10 minutes until almost tender.

Grease a gratin dish with butter and spread the beans evenly over the bottom. Mix the crème fraîche, double cream, salt, pepper and a scraping or two of freshly grated nutmeg. Pour the mixture evenly over the beans and bake at 200°C (180°C if using a fan oven) or Gas Mark 6 for 20 minutes. Sprinkle the cheeses over the hot beans and brown under a hot grill or put back in the oven until golden brown and bubbling. Very good with plain grilled meats or roasts.

# Oriental-style mangetout

2 tablespoons groundnut or sunflower oil
2½cm (1 inch) peeled, grated fresh ginger
1 large crushed clove of garlic
4 thinly sliced spring onions
A pinch of chilli powder
2 tablespoons dark soy sauce
300g (10oz) trimmed mangetout

Heat the oil in a wide pan. Gently fry the ginger, garlic and spring onions until the onion is soft. Add the pinch of chilli powder and soy sauce.

Steam the mangetout for 4 minutes until just softening. Tip them into the sauce and stir-fry for 1–2 minutes until the mangetout are tender and coated with sauce.

These are particularly good with fish or can be used with other Chinese dishes.

# Peas and beans in mustard sauce

**10g (½oz) butter**
**1 finely chopped shallot**
**200g (7oz) French beans cut in half across**
**200g (7oz) shelled fresh or frozen peas**
**5 tablespoons crème fraîche**
**5 tablespoons double cream**
**1½ tablespoons Dijon mustard**
**Salt and freshly ground black pepper**

Melt the butter in a medium-sized pan and gently fry the shallot for about 5 minutes until it starts to colour.

Steam the beans for 7 minutes until "al dente". Boil the peas in a small amount of water for 2 minutes. Drain, reserving the water for stock.

Mix the crème fraîche, double cream and mustard together. Add the cooked shallot and butter. Season with salt and pepper to taste and pour over the vegetables.

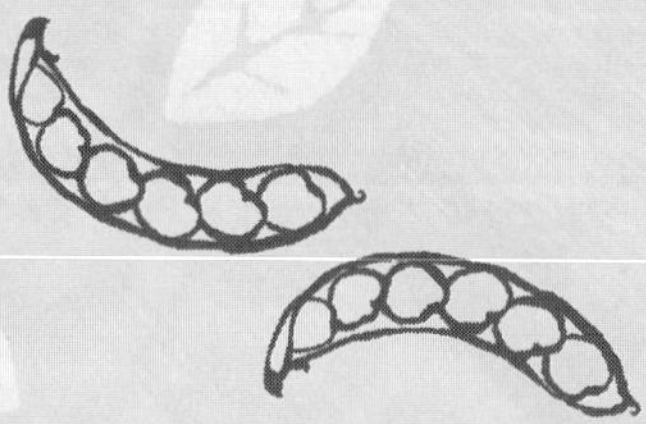

# Salads

# Gloria's green bean salad

This is a recipe given to me by a Chilean friend of mine. It is so simple and yet so delicious.

**150g (5oz) trimmed French beans**
**8 quartered cherry tomatoes**
**6 thinly sliced spring onions**
**A small handful of coriander or parsley**
**1 tablespoon lemon juice**
**3 tablespoons olive oil**
**Salt and pepper**

Steam the beans for 5–8 minutes until just cooked. Combine beans, tomatoes, onions and chosen herb in a bowl. Whisk the lemon juice, oil and seasoning together. Pour over the bean mixture and toss.

# Green bean and olive salad

250g (9oz) trimmed runner beans cut across into bite-sized diamond pieces
16 stoned kalamata black olives
2 thinly sliced medium shallots
3 tablespoons extra virgin olive oil
Lemon juice to taste
Salt and pepper

Steam the beans for 8–10 minutes until "al dente". Rinse in cold water.

Combine the beans with the other ingredients and toss well.

# French bean and mushroom salad with sherry vinaigrette

**300g (10oz) young French beans**
**A bunch of spring onions**
**2 tablespoons sunflower oil**
**1 crushed medium-sized clove of garlic**
**200g (7oz) unpeeled button mushrooms**

**For the dressing:**

**2 tablespoons sherry vinegar**
**1 tablespoon red wine vinegar**
**1½ tablespoons walnut oil**
**120ml (4fl oz) extra virgin olive oil**
**Sea salt and freshly ground black pepper**

Cook the beans in boiling salted water for 5 minutes or until softened but still with a slight crunch.

Trim and slice the white and pale green parts of the spring onions. Heat the sunflower oil over a medium heat and stir-fry the onions and garlic for a couple of minutes. Remove the onions and garlic to a salad bowl and add the beans. Turn the heat to high and use the same frying pan to sauté the mushrooms for about 2 minutes until they start to colour but before the juices start to run. Add to the bean mixture.

Make the dressing by whisking all the ingredients together. Pour it over the bean mixture, toss thoroughly and serve.

# Herby French bean salad

200g (7oz) trimmed French beans
4 tablespoons crème fraîche
1 tablespoon lemon juice
1 teaspoon Dijon mustard
Sea salt and freshly ground pepper
3 tablespoons of your very best extra virgin olive oil
A handful of finely chopped mixed herbs
(chives, tarragon and thyme are a good combination)
Chopped chives to garnish

Steam the beans until tender, refresh in cold water and cut across into bite-sized pieces.

To make the dressing, put the crème fraîche into a bowl. Stir in the lemon juice, Dijon mustard and seasoning, then whisk in the olive oil. Stir in the herbs.

Dress the beans with the herb dressing, garnish with a few chopped chives. Leave for 30 minutes to allow the flavours to develop before serving.

# Screwy pasta, bacon and green bean salad

**350g (12oz) corkscrew or other twisted pasta**
**200g (7oz) smoked bacon lardons**
**225g (8oz) French beans cut into matchsticks**
**12 cherry tomatoes**
**Chopped white parts of a bunch of spring onions**

**For the dressing:**

**1 teaspoon Dijon mustard**
**1 tablespoon balsamic vinegar**
**2 tablespoons white wine vinegar**
**75ml (3fl oz) sunflower oil**
**75ml (3fl oz) extra virgin olive oil**
**Salt and pepper**
**A handful of roughly chopped basil leaves**

Boil the pasta until "al dente", according to the instructions on the packet. Stir-fry the lardons over a high heat until some of the fat has drained out and they are going brown. Drain and cool on kitchen paper.

Boil the beans for about 5 minutes until nearly tender. Drain, reserving the water for stock. Halve the cherry tomatoes.

Mix all the salad ingredients together in a salad bowl.

Make the dressing by beating all but the basil together vigorously. Stir in the basil and pour over the salad. Mix well and serve.

# Salad of peas, cherry tomatoes and ricotta

**250g (9oz) fresh young peas or frozen petits pois**
**100g (3½oz) ricotta cheese**
**1 tablespoon olive oil**
**50g (2oz) peeled, thinly sliced shallots**
**1 large peeled, thinly sliced clove of garlic**
**12 small halved cherry tomatoes**

**For the dressing:**

**1 tablespoon white balsamic condiment**
**2 tablespoons extra virgin olive oil**
**Salt and pepper**

Cook the peas gently in water for 2 minutes. Drain, reserving the cooking water for stock. Very carefully cut the ricotta into cubes. Don't worry if it doesn't hold together. You can crumble it over the salad instead.

Heat 1 tablespoon of olive oil and gently fry the shallots and garlic for 10 minutes until soft.

Whisk the balsamic condiment, oil, salt and freshly ground black pepper together for the dressing.

Mix the peas, fried shallots and garlic and cherry tomatoes in a salad bowl. Pour ¾ of the dressing over the mixture and toss. Put the ricotta on top and drizzle the rest of the dressing over it.

This salad is best served at room temperature, or even warm, but cut the ricotta when chilled so that it holds together better.

# Warm Greek salad of runner beans

**2 tablespoons extra virgin olive oil**
**2 teaspoons paprika pepper**
**A pinch of cayenne pepper**
**1 large, peeled and crushed clove of garlic**
**500g (18oz) topped, tailed and stringed runner beans**
**100ml (3½fl oz) water**
**Salt and freshly ground black pepper**
**I tablespoon extra virgin olive oil to finish**

Heat the oil in a medium-sized pan. Add the paprika and cayenne peppers and the garlic. Cook for 1 minute, then add the beans and water. Cover the pan and cook gently for 10 minutes. Remove the lid, turn up the heat and boil off the remaining water, by which time the beans should be soft. Allow to cool a little. Season well and add the tablespoon of olive oil.

I like this best warm but you can serve it cold if you prefer.

# Bushman's salad (or Jen's bean and pea salad)

Serves 6–8

**150g (5oz) halved green beans**
**150g (5oz) halved yellow beans**
**150g (5oz) fresh or frozen peas**
**80g (3oz) canned red kidney beans**
**80g (3oz) canned black beans**
**80g (3oz) canned chickpeas**
**2 thinly sliced spring onions including 5cm (2 inches) of the green part**
**1 tablespoon chopped flat-leaf parsley for garnish**

**For the dressing:**

**75ml (3fl oz) red wine vinegar**
**½ tablespoon Dijon mustard**
**½ teaspoon sugar**
**Salt and freshly ground black pepper**
**60ml (2fl oz) extra virgin olive oil**
**60ml (2fl oz) good quality mayonnaise**
**1 teaspoon finely chopped fresh thyme leaves**

Yellow beans can be hard to find so you can always use helda or other beans of your choice. Steam or blanch both beans leaving them crunchy. Cook the peas for 2 minutes, drain and cool.

Wash the canned beans and put them in a salad bowl. Add the blanched beans, peas and spring onions.

Make the dressing by whisking the vinegar, mustard, sugar, salt and pepper in a small bowl. Whisking constantly, add the oil in a slow, steady stream and continue whisking until thickened. Stir in the mayonnaise and chopped thyme.

Toss the salad with the dressing and sprinkle the chopped parsley on top.

# Mangetout, quail's egg, ricotta and tomato salad with chive dressing

3–4 quail's eggs per person
3 small cherry tomatoes per person
175g (6oz) trimmed mangetout
175g (6oz) good quality ricotta cheese, chilled
Some crunchy salad leaves or lettuce
Black pepper

**For the dressing:**

2 tablespoons lemon juice
50g (2oz) chopped chives
6 tablespoons extra virgin olive oil
Sea salt

This dish can be served both as a starter or salad.

Boil the quail's eggs for 2–3 minutes, depending on how firm you like them. Put into cold water to stop them cooking and allow them to get absolutely cold. Carefully shell the eggs under running cold water and keep them covered with water while you prepare the rest of the salad.

Wash and cut the tomatoes in half. Steam the mangetout for 4 minutes, leaving them a little crunchy. Plunge them into cold water to cool. Cut diagonally into bite-sized pieces. Gently cut the ricotta cheese into cubes.

Make the dressing by putting the lemon juice and chopped chives into a blender and whizz to chop the chives even more finely, then blend in the oil and season with a little sea salt.

Place the shredded salad leaves on four plates. Arrange the mangetout on top, then add the eggs, tomatoes and ricotta. Grind a little black pepper on top and pour some of the dressing over each salad. Serve with crusty bread.

# Mangetout, avocado and mushroom salad with clams

**300g (10oz) mangetout**
**1 large or two small avocado pears**
**300g (10oz) quartered button mushrooms**
**The juice of 1 lemon**
**75fl (3fl oz) extra virgin olive oil**
**Salt and freshly ground black pepper**
**A 300g (10oz) can of baby clams, drained**

Trim the mangetout and string them if necessary. Blanch for 1 minute, drain and plunge into cold water to refresh. Cut them in half across.

Drain the clams and rinse them well as they are always full of sand.

Halve and peel the avocado, remove the stone and dice the flesh. Put the cubes into a salad bowl together with the quartered button mushrooms and pour over the lemon juice over. Stir, covering the cubes with the juice. Add the mangetout and clams. Season with salt and freshly ground black pepper. Pour the olive oil over the salad and mix well. Leave to absorb the flavours before serving.

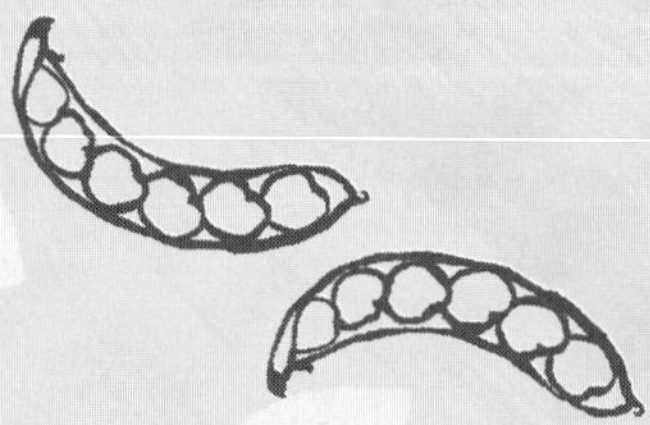

# Sundries

# Green bean and caramelised onion tartlets

**3 tablespoons water**
**½ teaspoon salt**
**Freshly ground black pepper**
**2 tablespoons unsalted butter**
**3 large, very thinly sliced onions**
**200g (7oz) trimmed French beans**
**1 pack ready rolled shortcrust pastry (or make your own)**
**A tablespoon of finely chopped chives**
**5 tablespoons crème fraîche**

Put the water, salt, pepper, butter and onion into a wide, heavy based pan. Cover and cook on a low heat for 10 minutes. Remove the lid and continue cooking, stirring frequently for about 25 minutes until the onion is a deep golden brown.

Steam the beans for 5–7 minutes, leaving them slightly crunchy. Cool and cut into 1½cm (approx. ¾ inch) lengths.

Roll out the pastry very thinly and cut into rounds. Line a mini muffin tray with the rounds to make the tartlets. Prick all over the pastries and bake at 200°C (180°C if using a fan oven) or Gas Mark 6 for 10 minutes until cooked through and golden. Cool.

Mix the chives into the crème fraîche and put a teaspoonful in the bottom of each tartlet. Top with the caramelised onion and pieces of bean.

# Pea puree

**500g (18oz) shelled fresh or frozen peas**
**25g (1oz) roughly chopped fresh mint leaves**
**100g (3½oz) curd cheese**
**A little lemon juice**

Cook the peas until tender. Drain and pour into a food processor or blender together with the mint. Add the curd cheese and a squeeze of lemon juice and whizz to a puree. This won't be entirely smooth but that doesn't matter.

You can use this as a filling for cocktail bites or cannelloni. It is in my recipes for Pea and prawn roulade (p.32), Pea soufflé (p.35) and Pea custards with tomato sauce (p.36). You can adapt it by adding other flavours for a dip or spread. It also freezes well.

# Jen's sweet pea puree in endive spears

This is a lovely recipe for a drinks party, given to me by my dear, amazingly talented American friend, Jennifer Bushman, who has inspired and supported me during the creation of these recipes.

**120ml (4fl oz) extra virgin olive oil**
**2 tablespoons butter**
**1 small seeded and chopped hot red chilli pepper**
**1 tablespoon chopped mint leaves**
**2 crushed medium cloves of garlic**
**375g (13oz) fresh or frozen young peas**
**A pinch sugar**
**175g (6oz) ricotta cheese**
**Salt and freshly ground black pepper**
**4 endive heads, washed and separated into spears**

Heat the oil, butter, chilli and mint in a heavy medium pan over a medium heat for 2 minutes. Add the garlic and stir for 1 minute. Stir in the peas and sugar. Cook for about 5 minutes until the peas are just tender. Reserve a few peas for garnishing.

Transfer the pea mixture to a food processor and puree until almost smooth (some texture should remain). Add the ricotta and puree for a few seconds to combine. Season to taste with salt and pepper.

Either pipe or spoon 1 tablespoon of the mixture into the bottom third of the endive spear. Garnish with a pea and a small mint leaf.

# Italian flag canapés

**Cherry tomatoes**
**Horseradish sauce**
**A little cream**
**Curd cheese**
**French beans cooked "al dente"**

It is impossible to give quantities for this. It all depends on how many people you are catering for. At a drinks party with other canapés you should provide 2–3 of these for each person.

Cut the tops off the tomatoes or halve them if they are large. Scoop out the centres with a coffee spoon, sprinkle with a little salt and turn them upside down on kitchen paper to drain for 30 minutes.

Mix a very small amount of horseradish and a little cream into the curd cheese to make a soft cheese mixture. Cut the French beans across into small lengths.

Stuff the tomatoes with the cheese mixture. You may find it easier to use a piping bag. Push the beans vertically into the centres, leaving some green sticking up (about 4 sticks per tomato.) A very pretty and popular canapé.

# Broad bean pod puree

When you have a large amount of young broad beans to shell (at least 2 kilos or 4lbs 4oz), the pods make a very useful puree. You really need a Mouli vegetable mill for this. If you haven't got one, you can push the cooked pods through a strong strainer with a wooden spoon.

Put a very large pan full of water on to boil. Wash the beans thoroughly and cut off any stalky and black bits. Plunge the pods into the boiling water and cook them for about 15 minutes until they are very tender.

Drain, and put them into a bath of cold water. Drain again, squeezing out as much water as possible.

Use the finest Mouli sieve to puree the pods, then season them with salt, lemon juice and black pepper. This puree can be made into a dip, a soup, a spread, or any number of other uses.

# Runner bean chutney

**1kilo (2lbs 2oz) runner beans cut into diamond pieces and steamed until tender**
**1kilo (2lbs 2oz) peeled and roughly chopped cooking apples**
**1kilo (2lbs 2oz) peeled and roughly chopped onions**
**1 quartered and thinly sliced lemon**
**700ml (1¼ pints) cider vinegar**
**450g (1lb) soft light brown muscovado sugar**
**1 teaspoon turmeric**
**1 tablespoon salt**

**For the spice bag:**

**The peel and core of the apples**
**1 teaspoon coriander seeds**
**½ teaspoon cumin seeds**
**1 teaspoon black peppercorns**
**1 teaspoon fenugreek seeds**
**4 cloves**
**1-2 dried red chillies**
**2½cm (1 inch) crushed cinnamon stick**

I find this recipe works best with freshly steamed beans, rather than raw ones.

Line a small pudding basin with a piece of muslin 30cm (12 inches) square. Put all the ingredients for the spice bag into the basin, gather the muslin edges together to form a parcel and tie with kitchen string. This saves the seeds running all over the place if you try to do it flat!

Put all the chutney ingredients, apart from the turmeric and salt, into a preserving pan. Bury the spice bag in the pot and bring to the boil. Stir until the sugar has dissolved and then simmer the mixture for about 50 minutes until thickened.

Leave to cool overnight. Check that the cold mixture is thick enough and bring back to the boil, cooking for a little longer if you are not happy with the consistency. Stir in the turmeric and salt. Fill hot sterilised jam jars with the hot chutney. (It should fill five.) Put waxed paper rings on top and seal with a well-fitting lid. The chutney should be ready to eat in one month.

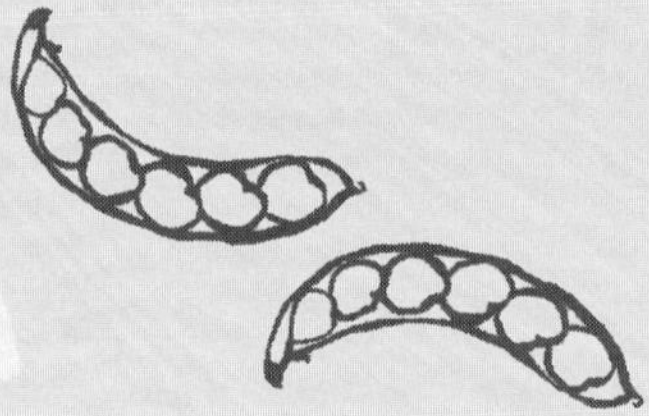

# Index of Recipes

# Index of Recipes